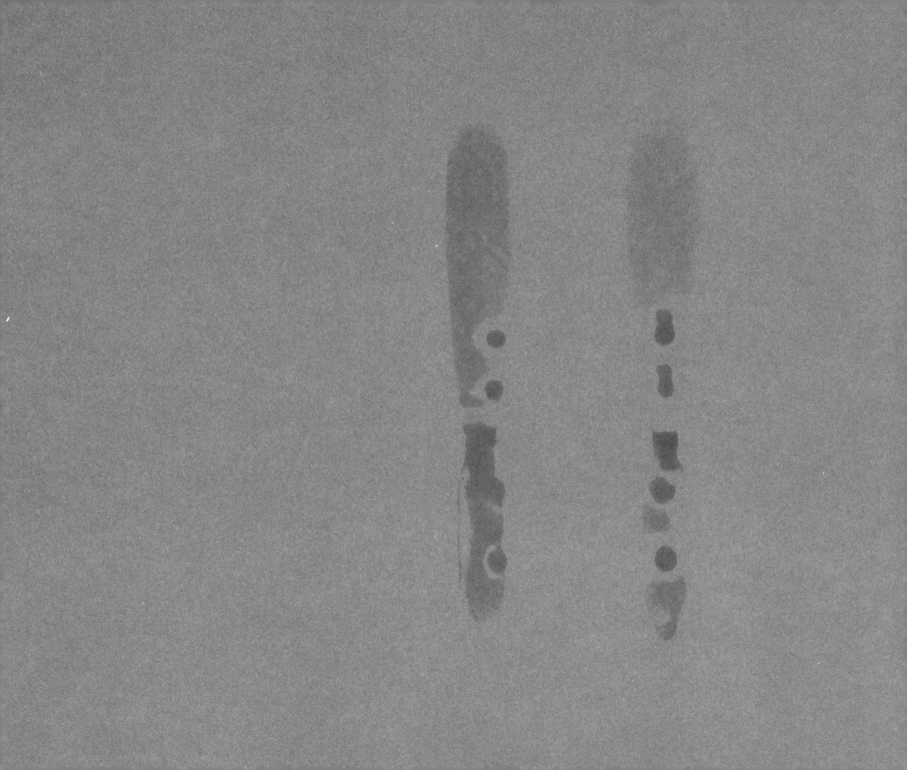

A Fisher

by Douglas Florian

Greenwillow Books New York

*Library of Congress
Cataloging-in-Publication Data*
Florian, Douglas.
A fisher / by Douglas Florian.
p.   cm.
ISBN 0-688-13129-8 (trade).
ISBN 0-688-13130-1 (lib. bdg.)
1. Fishers—Juvenile literature.
2. Fishing—Juvenile literature.
[1. Fishers. 2. Fishing. 3. Occupations.]
I. Title.   HD8039.F65F55   1994
331.7'6392—dc20
93-26515   CIP   AC

GRATEFUL ACKNOWLEDGMENT TO
CAPTAIN TIM SWANSON OF THE *ST. PETER*

For *SCH, ECS, AMW, & PL*

A fisher catches fish.

This fisher works from a small boat.

Early in the morning his boat pulls away from the dock and heads for the open ocean.

In the wheelhouse the fisher uses his special equipment to steer a course.

His compass tells him the direction
in which the boat is going.

His loran is a special radio that
tells him the boat's exact location.

His radar shows him if a
boat, buoy, or land is nearby.

His depth finder shows him the
ocean floor under the boat.

The fisher knows from experience the best times and locations to fish. When he arrives at a good place, he slows down the boat. Then he puts on his oilers, gloves, and sleeves to keep dry. As the boat continues slowly along, he drops the heavy net over the rail. This is called "setting out the net."

gloves

sleeves

oilers

boots

As the net, with its heavy chains, sinks to the bottom, the fisher increases the speed of the boat. The net is pulled along the sea floor, or "trawled," by the boat. Any boat or ship that catches fish in this way is called a trawler.

After about two hours the net is full of fish and crabs and ready to be hauled back.

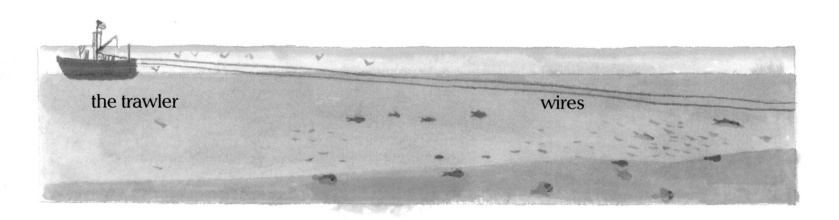

the trawler   wires

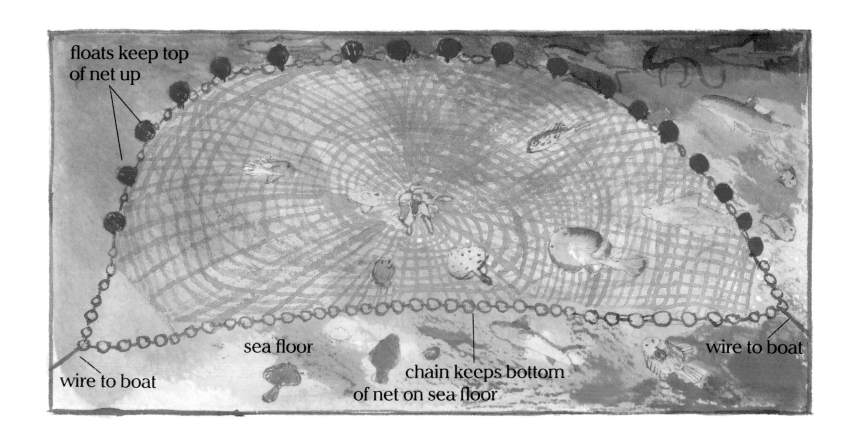

floats keep top
of net up

sea floor

wire to boat

chain keeps bottom
of net on sea floor

wire to boat

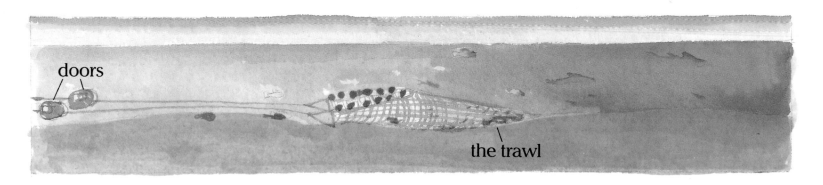

doors

the trawl

A strong motor called a winch pulls the net from the sea floor to the surface. Then with a rope and pulley the fisher hoists the net above the deck.

Once the net is in place, the fisher tugs it open, and the catch of fish and crabs pours out onto the deck.

black sea bass

northern
kingfish

weakfish

He sorts the fish he can sell into baskets.
This is known as "picking the deck."

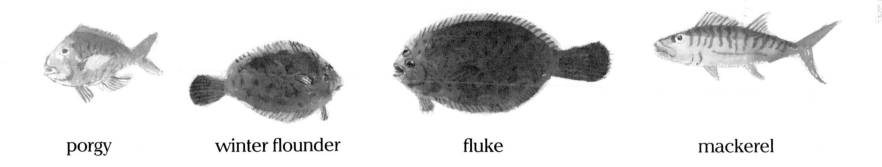

porgy   winter flounder   fluke   mackerel

After he has picked the deck, the fish and crabs that remain are pushed back into the sea through openings in the rail called scuppers.

blue crab

baby shark

eel

helmet crab

sea robin

skate

He hoses down the deck and then is ready to set out the net again. In one trip the fisher may set out and haul back the net five or more times.

After many hours of hard work the fisher heads back to the dock with his catch.

At the dock there is more work for the fisher. With the help
of his dock worker he unloads the baskets of fish.
The fish are washed and weighed, then put into boxes.

Crushed ice keeps the fish fresh while the fisher makes any needed repairs to his boat or net.

Later, in the night, the fisher trucks his boxes of freshly caught fish to a big fish market in the city. There he sells them to fish vendors.

In the morning, when the market opens to the public, the fish vendors start selling the fish to buyers from restaurants and neighborhood fish markets, and to the general public.

Day or night,

rain or shine,

stern trawler

shrimp trawler

salmon fishing boat

oyster dredger

from a small boat or from a big ship,

a fisher catches fish.

TODAY MOST FISHERS WORK TO HELP CONSERVE THE SUPPLY OF FISH IN THE OCEAN. THEY USE NETS WITH A WIDE MESH THAT ALLOW SMALLER, OFTEN YOUNGER, FISH TO ESCAPE. THEY DON'T FISH IN SPAWNING GROUNDS, THE PLACES WHERE FISH RELEASE THEIR EGGS. THEY DON'T FISH FOR THE KINDS OF FISH THAT ARE IN VERY SHORT SUPPLY. AND THEY DON'T FISH FOR SEA MAMMALS, SUCH AS WHALES OR DOLPHINS. THEY HOPE THESE AND OTHER MEASURES WILL HELP TO KEEP THE OCEANS FULL OF FISH IN THE YEARS TO COME.

A FISHER'S EQUIPMENT

Hollow metal or plastic balls called floats raise the top of the net off the ocean floor.

A spotlamp lights up the deck at night or in fog or rain.

Wooden boxes called fish wells store large amounts of fish at sea.

Openings in the boat's rail called scuppers allow water to run off.

Gloves and sleeves keep the fisher's hands and arms dry.

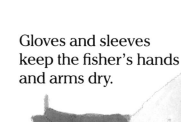

A strong motor called a winch lets the net sink down and pulls the net up.

Oilers, also known as oilskins, keep the fisher's legs and waist dry.

A wheel steers the boat. The wooden pegs are easy to hold with wet hands.

Two heavy metal plates called doors help to keep the net spread open on the sea floor.

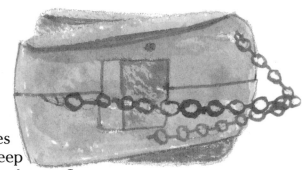